The TIME *trekkers* visit the STONE AGE

ANTONY MASON

COPPER BEECH BOOKS
BROOKFIELD, CONNECTICUT

Designed and produced by
Aladdin Books Ltd
28 Percy Street
London W1P 0LD

First published in
the United States in 1996 by
Copper Beech Books,
an imprint of
The Millbrook Press
2 Old New Milford Road
Brookfield, Connecticut 06804

Editor
Jim Pipe
Designed by
David West Children's Books
Designer
Simon Morse
Illustrated by
Sheena Vickers
Additional illustrations by
Ian Thompson
David Burroughs

Printed in Belgium

Library of Congress Cataloging-in-Publication Data
Mason, Antony.
The Stone Age / by Antony Mason: illustrated by Sheena Vickers and Dave Burroughs.
p. cm. -- (The time trekkers visit --)
Includes index.
ISBN 0-7613-0479-7 (lib. bdg.).--
ISBN 0-7613-0480-0 (pbk.)
1. Stone age--Juvenile literature. 2. Man, Prehistoric--Juvenile literature. I. Vickers, Sheena, ill. II. Burroughs, Dave, 1952- ill. III. Title. IV. Series: Time trekkers visit the--
GN768. M37 1996 95-39833
930. 1'2--dc20 CIP AC

CONTENTS

Introduction

The Time trekkers are Lucy, Jools, Eddie, and Sam. Using the time machine invented by Lucy's eccentric grandfather, they travel through time and space on amazing voyages of discovery. Their gizmos are always ready to answer any questions!

But before we follow their journey back to the Stone Age, let's meet the four adventurers...

The Time Trekkers

Lucy – As she is the oldest of the four travelers, Lucy gets a bit bossy at times. But when the going gets tough, the others rely on her to save the day.

Jools – is always in a rush to get somewhere, but when he stops he usually gets caught up in the local wildlife. His pet frog, Kevin, isn't always easy to find.

Eddie – With his knowledge of history, it's Eddie's job to set the controls on the time machine. But he does have a tendency to drift off into a dreamworld!

Sam – When the time machine starts acting up, call Sam, the Time trekkers' research scientist. She's a whiz with all kinds of gadgets, but she gets so wrapped up in her Walkman that she often doesn't notice the danger around her!

The Gizmo

To use this gizmo, simply read the Time trekkers' question bubbles, then look to the gizmo for the answer! There are three subject buttons:

- *Science (Orange)*
- *Places and People (Purple)*
- *History and Arts (Red)*

And two extra special functions:

- *X ray (Yellow)*
- *Translator (Blue)*

What a great vacation. The Time trekkers were in the Dordogne region of southwest France. Here they spent lazy days swimming in the rivers and cooking over a barbecue. But was this enough for the Time trekkers? No, they needed adventure!

So Jools' dad took them to see a prehistoric cave. The walls were covered in amazing paintings of animals, and that night, as they sat around the fire, Sam wondered, what it would be like to live there. "Why dream about it," said Jools, "when you can see for yourself. Last one to the time machine is a rotten egg!"

Why is it called the Stone Age?
STONE, BRONZE, AND IRON AGES
The early history of humans is divided up into periods that are named after the main materials which were used to make tools.
In the Stone Age, about 2.5 million–3,500 years B.C., stone tools (*top*) were used. During the Bronze Age, about 3,500–1,500 years B.C., better tools (*right*) were made of the metal bronze. In the Iron Age, about 1,500–800 years B.C., tools were made of iron (*left*).

How do we know about the Stone Age?
ARCHAEOLOGY
Stone Age people had not learned to write, so we do not have any written records of how they lived. A lot of what we know comes from things found by experts (called archaeologists) in the caves and other places where Stone Age people lived.
These include stone tools, jewelry made of bone, cave paintings, and skeletons. A great deal can be learned by digging up these places very carefully, using trowels, brushes, and tools (*right*).

EARLY HUMANS

Modern humans (*Homo sapiens*) only developed 100,000 years B.C. One of the first of our ancestors, *Australopithecus*, lived 4 million years B.C. By 2.5 million years B.C. they had evolved into *Homo habilis*.

Homo erectus, the people you're looking at, first appeared 2 million years B.C.

Australopithecus

Homo habilis

Homo erectus

Homo sapiens

OUR ORIGINS IN AFRICA

Homo erectus

You're in Africa, where 20th-century archaeologists will find the oldest human skeleton.

So perhaps this is where human life began. About now (1.8 million years B.C.), *Homo erectus* begins to move north into the Middle East, Europe, and Asia.

Eddie, exhausted by the race to the time machine, tapped in far too many zeros. "Oh no," he cried, "I've sent us back 1.8 million years!" As they landed, Sam let out a terrible scream. Squashed against the window was a big, hairy face! "I don't think he wants to hurt us," said Lucy. The others got out for a closer look, but Sam wasn't moving! Jools was also itching to leave, "Come on, let's go and see some *real* cave people."

Who are these people?
Where exactly are we?
What is he doing with that stone?

TOOLS

Homo habilis means "handy people." They are given this name because they were the first humans to make stone tools (*right*).

The larger-brained *Homo erectus* you are looking at now use tools to crush nuts and kill animals for food, while the points are sharp enough to cut meat.

With their sharper tools (*left*) and their increasingly big brain, *Homo erectus* will gradually become the dominant species in the animal world.

Eddie set the dials... the machine burst into action, and 1,782,000 years later, it skidded to a halt on a barren, icy plain.

The clock read *minus 20,000*, but when the Time trekkers looked out, there wasn't a single human being to be seen. All they saw was a landscape dotted with strange, large animals. What's more, it was bitter cold, and except for Eddie's chattering teeth, it was very quiet. Then they heard weird, frightening noises...

THE ICE AGES
At various times in the Earth's history the whole planet became much cooler. The ice caps at the poles became larger, and winters in the north and south became much colder and lasted longer. These periods of cold are called *Ice Ages*.
This Ice Age began about 100,000 years B.C., and will last another 10,000 years. The average winter temperature in northern Europe at this time is 12° F.
Ice Cap
But where are all the people?
MIGRATION
The world is still full of vast empty spaces, because there aren't many people yet.
Humans spread out from Africa over thousands of years, and by 40,000 years B.C. they had reached southern Asia and Australia. The sea level is lower during this Ice Age, and Alaska is joined to Russia by a "land bridge." People can now walk from Asia into North America.
Brrrrr! Why is it so cold?

Running to the crest of the hill, the Time trekkers saw a huge woolly mammoth that had gotten stuck in a bog. A group of men, dressed in skins and armed with spears, jumped down from the cliff. They let out blood-curdling screams, and rushed at the animal.

The mammoth fought back, stamping with its feet and slicing through the air with its huge tusks. It grabbed one of the hunters with its trunk, and hurled him to the ground.

Who are these people?
They won't be able to catch it, will they?
Do they always hunt here?

HOMO SAPIENS

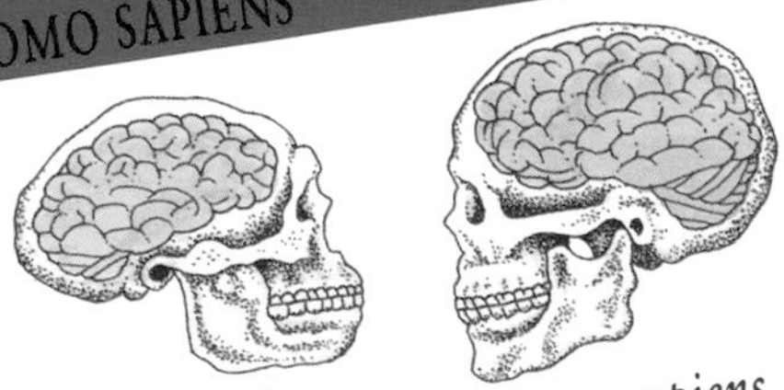

Homo erectus *Homo sapiens*

These are modern humans, *Homo sapiens* or "wise people," who first evolved from *Homo erectus* in about 100,000 B.C.

At each stage of evolution the human brain has become larger, so *Homo sapiens* have a larger brain than *Homo habilis*, for instance. But there is no reason to suggest these humans of 18,000 B.C. are less intelligent than later humans.

NOMADIC HUNTERS

These people live mainly by hunting. Many of the animals that they hunt, such as deer, move from one place to another during the seasons, in search of fresh food and water.

These hunters and their families follow the herds, so that they can be sure of good hunting. If they decide to stay for awhile in any place, they build huts and tents (*top*), or live in caves (*left*).

HUNTING METHODS

Stone Age hunters usually target smaller animals, such as deer, hares, and horses. They only attack mammoths from time to time if they are wounded, or as a challenge.

Snare

Their main weapons are spears with heads hardened by fire. They also use clubs, arrows shot from bows, and bolas (weights tied to string) for tripping up fleeing animals. Snares (*top*) are good for catching smaller prey.

Bolas

But after a fierce struggle, the hunters finally made their kill. Two stood guard, while the others cut the mammoth into sections. Suddenly, one of them stopped dead in his tracks. Sniffing the air, he walked toward where the Time trekkers were hiding.

The gang made a run for it, but in seconds they were surrounded by a ring of spears. "Hi guys," said Jools. "I'm Jools, and this is..." The hunters just shouted at the Time trekkers in a strange language, then marched them off to their camp.

TRIBES AND FAMILIES

These Stone Age people probably live in tribal groups. These consist mainly of people who are all related to each other in one way or another. It is highly likely that the tribes are led by chiefs.

Families may be loose-knit groups (*below*) rather than just a wife and husband and their children.

Is this some kind of tribe?
What are they saying?
Do they all live in tents?

LANGUAGE

No one knows what languages are spoken by these Stone Age people. *Homo sapiens* had had a large brain for some 80,000 years, so the chances are that language – a basic human skill – is not just a series of grunts, but fairly advanced.

Some early Stone Age carvings (*top*) show series of organized dots which may represent complex ideas such as calendars or even maps.

TENTS AND HUTS

Most Stone Age people do not stay in one place for long. They make temporary shelters out of whatever materials are at hand: skins, branches of trees, and reeds.

In some places, where there are a large number of mammoths, they make huts out of the bones of dead mammoths, covered with skins (*top*). It is wrong to think that most Stone Age people live in caves.

The leaders of the tribe inspected the Time trekkers. They looked at their smooth, clean skin, and touched their clothes. There was a lot of shouting and pointing, and the Time trekkers were terrified. "Just smile," said Lucy, "show them that we are friendly." It seemed to work and soon they were chatting with the aid of their gizmo translators.

Night came and it turned even colder. The tribe huddled around a fire, where a large piece of deer meat was being roasted. Suddenly, there was a loud roar – and a huge tiger leaped out of the darkness!

Lucky we've got fire!
W-w-what is *that*?

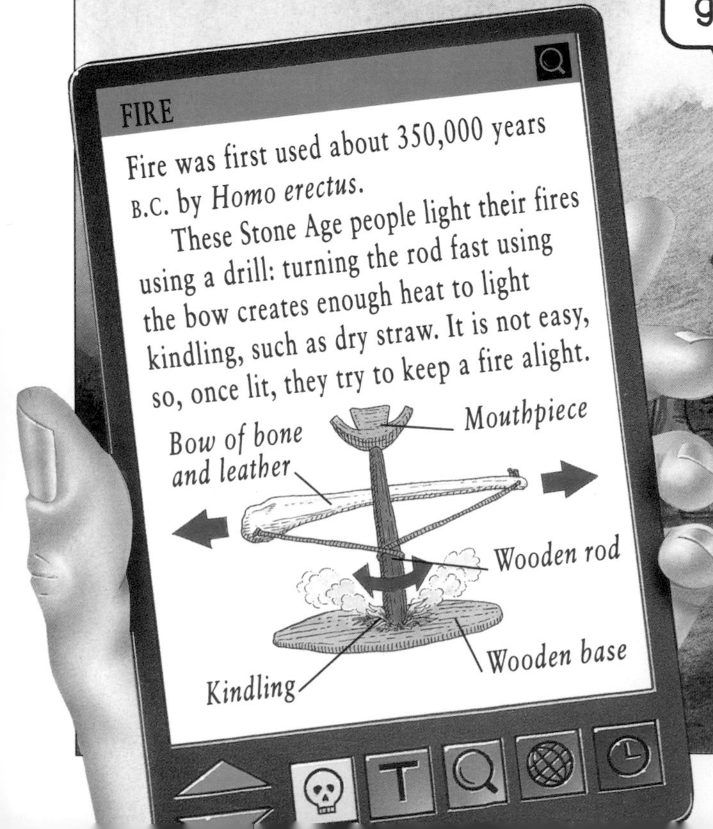

FIRE
Fire was first used about 350,000 years B.C. by *Homo erectus*.
These Stone Age people light their fires using a drill: turning the rod fast using the bow creates enough heat to light kindling, such as dry straw. It is not easy, so, once lit, they try to keep a fire alight.
Mouthpiece
Bow of bone and leather
Wooden rod
Wooden base
Kindling

DANGEROUS ANIMALS

Saber-toothed tiger

Hyena

Leopard

People live in constant fear of the aggressive animals around them, which can attack at any moment. Human meat is as good as any other, and fairly easy to catch!

Packs of hyenas prowl, killing any stragglers or weaklings, while the saber-toothed tiger is a deadly hunter.

The tribe chased the giant cat away by shouting and waving their flaming torches. When everyone eventually settled down for the night, the Time trekkers were allowed into one of the huts. Here they slept beneath a pile of soft furs. "They're even smellier than Eddie's feet," laughed Jools.

In the morning, the Time trekkers were given some nuts and

So what kind of things do these people eat?
Do they grow any of their own food?
STONE AGE FOOD
Hazelnuts
Juniper berries
Dandelion leaves
Birds' eggs
Fish
Mint
Wild wheat seeds
Meat
T
HUNTER-GATHERERS
These Stone Age people live by hunting animals for meat (*right*), and gathering wild fruits, leaves, and berries (*below*). People who live in this way are called "hunter-gatherers."
It is possible that some people grow crops by scattering seed in places where they know they will return. But farming as a way of life will take place only in about 8,000 years from now, in 10,000 B.C.
T

berries and some water from a leather bag. Later, they joined the others in the hunt for more food. They passed by a river, where the tribe fished with nets and spears. It seemed a good life, but it was hard to relax knowing that a saber-toothed tiger could pounce at any moment!

What are their nets made of?
Harpoons
Net

FISHING

Stone Age people fish using nets made of woven plant fibers or strips of leather. They also use harpoons with jagged heads carved from bone, to grip the fish when it's speared.

Fish are also caught by placing bait in basketlike traps made of woven willow branches.

As with meat, fresh fish can be dried in the sun for later use.

When they had filled their leather pouches with roots and berries, the children headed back to camp. Here a man was making clothes, sewing skins together with a bone needle. A woman was carving a little sculpture, and another was making a necklace of beads. Sam was amazed at their skills in carving.

The people worked quietly together, talking and laughing. But when a terrible wailing sound echoed around the valley, everyone stopped working, and walked toward the noise.

How do they make their tools?
What sort of clothes can they make?
Awl (for making holes)
Needle

CLOTHES AND MAKE-UP

Clothes are made mainly out of skin and fur. The pieces can be cut to shape and sewn together using needles made of bone, and thread made of strips of hide or the sinews of animals.

Weaving and cloth come later, in about 12,000 years! People like to decorate themselves with bright body paint (*right*).

MAKING STONE AGE TOOLS

Hard stone, such as flint, can be chipped away to form a sharp edge or point (*above*).

These sharpened stones are then bound with strips of leather to wooden shafts or handles to make knives, spears, and arrows. Other tools and weapons are made of bone, antlers, and wood.

JEWELRY AND CARVING

Necklace with the claws of a large cat

Stone Age people like to put on jewelry. They make beads and bangles out of bone, seeds, and animal teeth, and head-dresses out of flowers and feathers.

They are also skilled carvers, making statues of horses and humans.

Female figure made of stone

The Time trekkers followed the tribe to the bottom of a cliff. Here a young boy was being buried in his best clothes, with flowers and jewelry. Everyone was gathering to say their last farewell.

Beside the grave knelt a man covered in mysterious painted patterns. Clearly he was a priest or a witch doctor. When he saw the Time trekkers, he began to shout at them. It seemed that he was blaming the strangers for the boy's death. "I think we'd better go," whispered Lucy.

HUMAN BURIALS

The first human burials known were carried out about 100,000 years B.C., and it has been a ritual ever since.

Over time, burials have become increasingly elaborate. Some people believe that the dead will need clothes, weapons, and other possessions in the afterlife, and so bury them with such things. When several people in a family die at the same time, they are sometimes buried together in one grave (*right*).

SICKNESS AND HEALTH

Stone Age people suffer many of the illnesses we have today. We know this from the skeletons that have been found.

Ritual dance

They have little knowledge of medicine, but have learned to use certain herbs as natural cures. Catnip and rue, for instance, may be used to cure colds and headaches.

Catnip

They also try magic (*top*), and sometimes turn to primitive surgery.

Rue

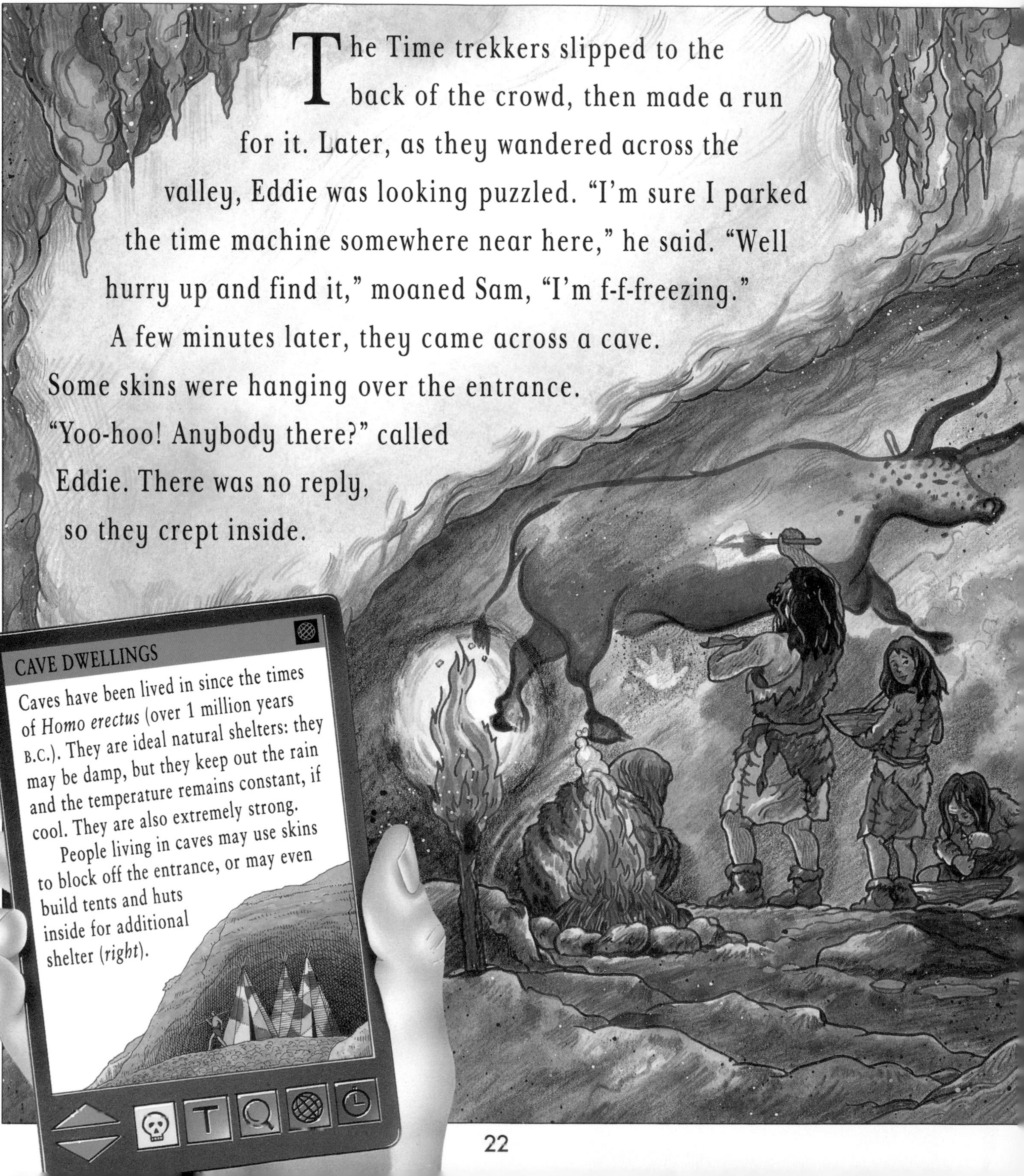

The Time trekkers slipped to the back of the crowd, then made a run for it. Later, as they wandered across the valley, Eddie was looking puzzled. "I'm sure I parked the time machine somewhere near here," he said. "Well hurry up and find it," moaned Sam, "I'm f-f-freezing."

A few minutes later, they came across a cave. Some skins were hanging over the entrance. "Yoo-hoo! Anybody there?" called Eddie. There was no reply, so they crept inside.

CAVE DWELLINGS

Caves have been lived in since the times of *Homo erectus* (over 1 million years B.C.). They are ideal natural shelters: they may be damp, but they keep out the rain and the temperature remains constant, if cool. They are also extremely strong.

People living in caves may use skins to block off the entrance, or may even build tents and huts inside for additional shelter (*right*).

It was very dark, but as their eyes got used to the light, a familiar sight greeted them. The walls were covered with paintings – magnificent pictures of animals, full of life and color, just like those they had seen before.

What is their paint made from?
Do they paint only animals?
Ah! Some real cave people!
Brush

CAVE PAINTINGS

Animals are the main subject of cave art. The animals depicted include horses (*above*), reindeer (*below*), woolly mammoths, and bison (*bottom*).

It is not certain why Stone Age artists paint the walls with animal pictures. Perhaps it is to help them with their hunting. Some paintings include spears and hunters.

PAINTS AND BRUSHES

Paints (*left*) are made from natural materials, such as charcoal (black) and soft rocks containing iron oxide (red). By heating iron oxide, a variety of colors from yellow to purple are made.

The brushes may be made of fur. Sometimes artists use a kind of spray gun: they fill their mouths with liquid paint, then spit it out!

Clunk! The silence of the cave was shattered by the sound of Sam dropping her Walkman. The artists whirled around, furious that anyone had dared to enter their cave. But the Time trekkers were already on their way out, slipping and sliding across the icy cave floor.

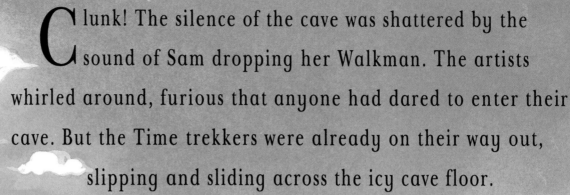

Why are some people staying?
Where are the others going?

STAYING IN ONE PLACE

The members of this tribe who are staying behind believe that there will be enough food for them all year-around.
Perhaps the camp is near a regular route taken by migrating animals.
When people begin to settle, they will have more time for new inventions. By 10,500 B.C. they will be making clay pots, and by 3,500 B.C. they will be using bronze (*above*) and will have invented the wheel (*left*).

They scrambled to the top of the hill, only to find another tribe in the valley below. They were surrounded! But Lucy noticed that the camp was in turmoil. Half of the tribe had packed up and was heading south, while the rest seemed to be staying behind.

HUMAN MIGRATION

Most hunter-gatherers are constantly on the move. This is how humans will cross over the land bridge from Asia to America: by following the herds of horses, bison, and deer. This will not happen at once, but even if a tribe moves only 30 miles a year, it will move 3,000 miles in 100 years.

Lucy decided that it was time for them to move on as well. It was cold and they were hungry. Besides, they were curious to see the first proper towns, and that meant heading 10,000 years into the future. Eddie finally remembered where the time machine was, and off they went!

They found themselves in the Middle East. It was wonderfully warm. There were houses, fields of crops, and herds of animals. There were even pottery jars being used to collect water from a spring. It beat drinking from a smelly leather bag!

DOMESTIC ANIMALS

Stone Age hunters have learned how to rear wild animals. They've found that they can take a young animal and keep it in a pen. Then they can kill it when they need it.

Dogs are also being tamed about this time. They help with the hunting.

THE FIRST HOUSES

The walls are built with bricks made out of a mixture of mud and straw dried in the sun. Wooden beams are placed across the tops of the walls then covered with a layer of mud to make a hard flat roof. The front door to each house is on the roof, reached by ladders!

Pottery is also made of baked clay. It is used to produce containers and dishes, and the bread ovens found inside the houses (*right*).

THE FIRST CROPS

The first crops, probably barley and wheat, grew wild. Hunter-gatherers collected them to make flour for bread.

Then they found that they could sow the seeds themselves. By keeping the best grains for planting, they learned to produce a better crop (*right*).

Well, things were clearly advancing fast in the world! But even having seen the Stone Age and the first villages, Jools still wasn't satisfied. So he persuaded the others to make one final trip – into the age of metal!

Eddie hit the dials once more. *Time: Minus 5,000.* Whoosh! Whizz! Sputter! They zapped on through the centuries, ending up in the same place where the Stone Age village had stood. But now things were rather different. It was 3000 B.C., and the Bronze Age had arrived.

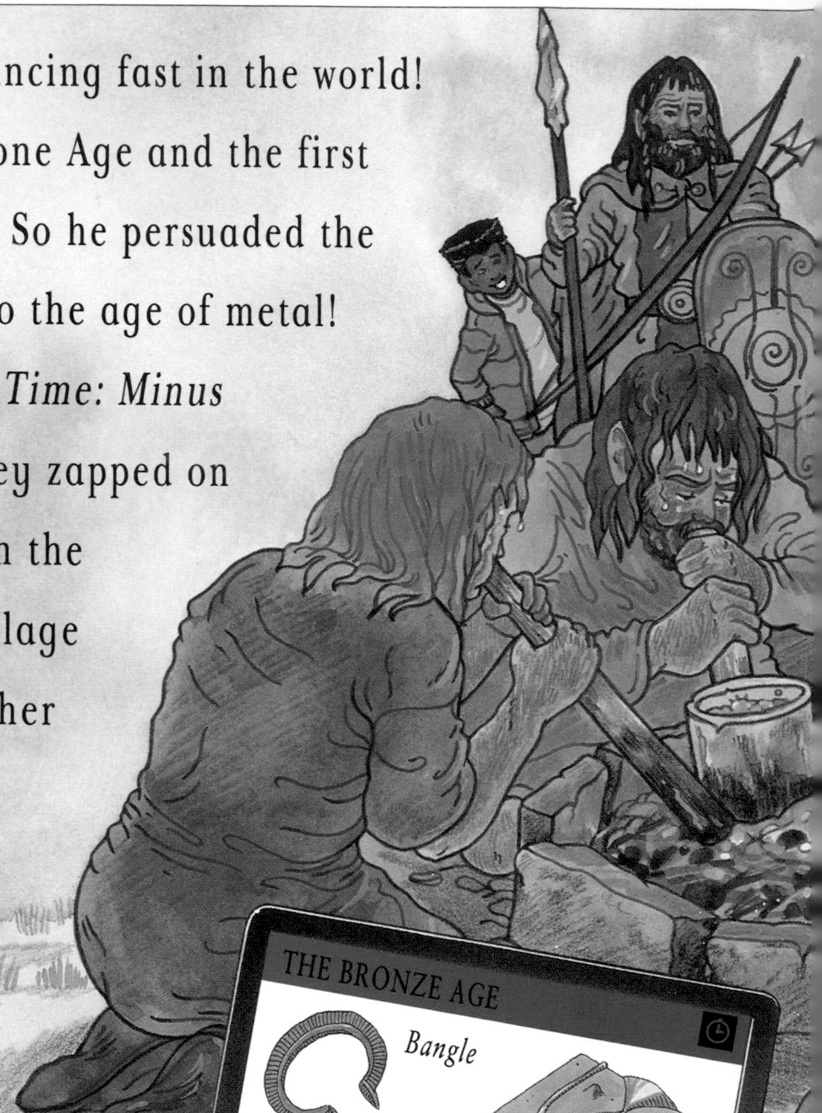

BRONZE

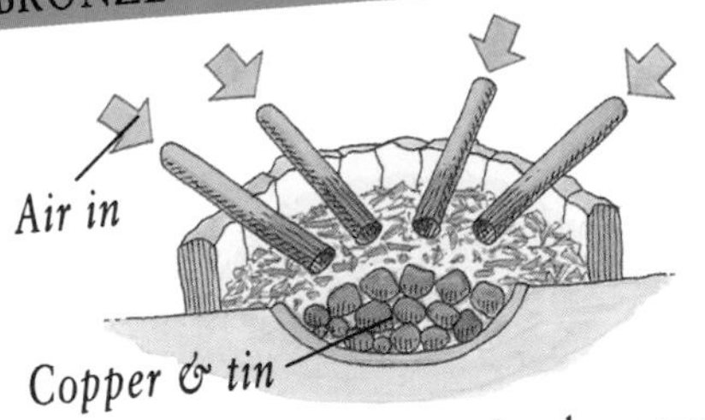

Since 10,000 B.C., copper has been used to make jewelry, but it is too soft for good tools. In about 3,500 B.C., however, smiths in the Middle East found that if they mixed copper with tin, it became much stronger.

They worked out that if air is blown into the furnace (using pipes), it makes the fire hot enough to melt the metals. The molten bronze is then poured into molds.

THE BRONZE AGE

Tools made from bronze are tougher and sharper than any made of stone. They can also be made quickly using molds. Bronze is used to make weapons, armor, and jewelry.

What is bronze? Why couldn't anyone use it before?
So was this the end of the Stone Age?
Why is bronze better for tools than stone?
THE MODERN STONE AGE
The whole world will not suddenly begin using bronze.
In many parts of the world, life will remain unchanged for centuries, and hunter-gatherers will exist until the 20th century in Australia, Southern Africa, and South America.
In the late 20th century there will still be some civilizations without metals (top). Usually they will live in areas cut off from the rest of the world, such as jungles.

The Time trekkers were beginning to feel rather weary. They had, after all, voyaged through nearly two million years of history. "Homeward bound!" said Eddie, and in seconds they had returned to the campsite.

They were glad to be back in their own modern world of electricity, running water, and cars. But when they looked back on their trip to the Stone Age, they realized that maybe people hadn't changed that much.

"After all," said Lucy, "what are we doing on vacation – living in tents, cooking food over a fire, and enjoying the fresh air – just like our Stone Age friends did."

THE GIZMO PUZZLER

1. The Time trekkers have a lucky escape from a saber-toothed tiger. How many other prehistoric animals can you find?

2. On page 14 Sam says "We're lucky we've got fire." Can you find what different uses fire has at the various stages of the adventure?

3. There are many different kinds of weapons and tools shown in this book. Can you find them all?

4. Can you spot Jools' frog, Kevin?

THE ANSWERS — JUST TURN THE BOOK UPSIDE DOWN AND LOOK AT IT IN A MIRROR!

1 Mammoths, giant bisons, woolly rhinoceroses, giant deer, musk oxen, hares (pages 8-9); mammoth (10-11); leopard, hyena (15); horses, butterfly, fish (16-17); horse (24-25); cows, dogs, pigs, goats, and sheep (26-27).

2 To harden wooden spears (gizmos on 11); to give light and warmth and to scare off animals (14-15); to cook food (18-19); for light (22-23); to make pottery and bake bread (26-27); to make bronze (28-29).

3 Stones to cut meat and crush nuts (6-7, 12); wooden spears (10, 11, 12, 13, 14, 20, 25); bolas and snares (10-11); tool for making fire (14); nets and harpoons, knives to cut corn (16-17); stone tools to cut and scrape leather, needles for sewing, instruments, (18-20), paintbrushes (22), bronze tools, shields, spearheads, and arrowheads, swords (28-29).

4 On the rock (5); on Jools' shoulder (7); on Jools' head (13); watching the saber-toothed tiger (14); diving into the stream (17); in Jools' pocket (16, 21); on the time machine (30).

2.4 million years B.C.
Homo habilis uses primitive stone tools.

1.8 million years B.C.
Homo erectus begins to move out of Africa.

100,000 years B.C.
Homo sapiens, the direct ancestor of modern humans.

40,000 years B.C.
Humans reach Australia.

20,000 years B.C. The first cave paintings, found mostly in France and Spain.

15,000 years B.C. The first humans migrate across the dry Bering Strait into North America.

10,000 years B.C. Copper is used in the Middle East.

9,000 years B.C. Humans begin to herd sheep.

8,000 years B.C. The beginnings of agriculture.

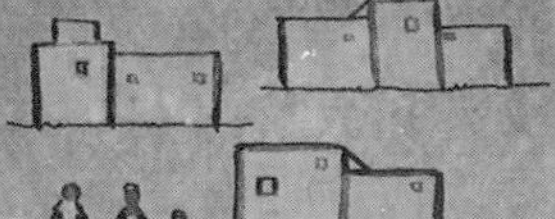

8,000 years B.C. Towns develop in the Middle East.

3,500 years B.C. Bronze is used in the Middle East.

3,500 years B.C. The invention of the wheel.